10 -

795R-5

THE KING PENGUIN BOOKS

UNKNOWN WESTMINSTER ABBEY

UNKNOWN WESTMINSTER ABBEY

BY LAWRENCE E. TANNER, M.V.O., F.S.A.
KEEPER OF THE MUNIMENTS AND LIBRARY
WESTMINSTER ABBEY
PHOTOGRAPHS BY R. P. HOWGRAVE-GRAHAM
F.S.A.

PENGUIN BOOKS
HARMONDSWORTH · MIDDLESEX
MCMXLVIII

THE KING PENGUIN BOOKS

EDITOR: N. B. L. PEVSNER · TECHNICAL EDITOR: R. B. FISHENDEN

PUBLISHED BY

PENGUIN BOOKS LIMITED, HARMONDSWORTH, MIDDLESEX, ENGLAND,
AND BY PENGUIN BOOKS PTY., LTD., 200, NORMANBY ROAD
MELBOURNE, AUSTRALIA

FIRST PUBLISHED 1948

TEXT PAGES PRINTED AT THE BAYNARD PRESS, LONDON, S.W.9
PLATES MADE AND PRINTED BY
CLARKE AND SHERWELL LIMITED, NORTHAMPTON
MADE IN GREAT BRITAIN

THE immediate predecessor of the present Abbey church of Westminster was built by Edward the Confessor about 1045 to 1065.[1] This great church which introduced the Norman-Romanesque style into England remained, as far as we know, unaltered, until a Lady Chapel was added to its east end in 1220. It was not long before greater ideas began to germinate in the mind of Henry III. What finally determined him to pull down the existing church and build the present Abbey church on its site is unknown. Tradition asserts that he had been deeply impressed by the beauty of Salisbury; it is not unlikely that the setting of the new shrine of Becket at Canterbury fired him with the desire to pay equal honour to the bones of the Confessor which were then interred in front of the High Altar at Westminster, and, if he had not already seen, he must have been told of the almost unbelievable beauty of the new cathedrals in northern France.

At any rate, the great work at Westminster was begun in 1245. It was the supreme hour of medieval art. All the great names – Chartres, Reims, Amiens, Beauvais, the Sainte Chapelle at Paris and the rest – belong to these decades. They came as a revelation; 'à peine pouvons-nous imaginer le charme qui rayonnait des cathédrales au temps de leur première jeunesse quand toutes les arêtes étaient vives, quand l'ornement gardait encore la blanche poussière du ciseau.'[2] Nor was this all; not only was Henry III a great patron of the arts himself, but he had at his side one who had profoundly studied these French cathedrals and had soaked himself in the new ideas to which they had given rise. Master Henry of Reynes, the king's master mason, whatever his nationality – and it is now pretty generally agreed that he was an Englishman – was a supreme genius who could not only appreciate all that was most lovely in French architecture of the time but could so 'rethink it into English idiom' as to evolve a building which was comparable in beauty with any which had arisen in France, and yet, to use the late Professor Lethaby's phrase, was 'triumphantly English' both in feeling and in detail.[3] Thus he seized on the lovely proportions of Amiens with its great main arches, its triforium, and its clerestory, but he gave to Westminster a triforium of definitely English design and of a peculiar beauty which makes the interior of Westminster so completely inevitable and satisfying.

In other instances, too, he was content to adapt freely from French models. Indeed for anyone who knows the Abbey intimately, a visit to Amiens, Reims, and other thirteenth-century French cathedrals is of absorbing interest, so constantly is one reminded of their influence on Westminster. Lethaby worked out these resemblances in detail, and he had no doubt that it is to Amiens primarily and then to Reims that we must look for the source from which our Westminster 'architect' took his inspiration.[4] Thus the deeply recessed porches in the North Front at Westminster, though they have been marred by restoration, were deliberately founded upon those of the West Front of Amiens; from Amiens, too, came the plan of the apse with its radiating chapels, although the actual form of those chapels with their pair-light windows reaching up to the vault, their wall arcades, and the wall passage which extends round the whole of the Abbey at this level is derived from Reims. The influence of Reims can be seen again in the natural and delightful way in which a window in one of the chapels on each side of the ambulatory fits into the vista of the side aisles of the nave and choir. There are other resemblances, too, such as the form of the pillars and of the tracery, and also the wooden and iron tie-bars which are so noticeable a feature at Westminster (Pl. 4). These last are contemporary with the building of the church and had their parallel at Reims. All these and other details will appeal to the trained eye of an architect. More generally the great rose-windows (Pl. 5) and the glorious flying buttresses (which are best seen from the cloister, Pl. 1) are essentially French features. But, while it is good to remember the debt we owe to France, it must be stressed again that Westminster was no mere copy. Again and again the man who conceived and built this great church showed his independence and gave full scope to his inventive genius. After all, and however interesting it may be to try to analyse French and English features, it is the church as it is – as it finally emerged from the hands of the builders – which is so inexhaustibly fascinating. It 'ever surprises by its loveliness' and no one, however familiar with it in all its varying moods, can ever go into it without seeing something fresh, some small point, it may be, of happy inspiration, some unexpected effect of light or shade, and those who know it best feel least confident that they have wrested from it the secrets which it guards.

7

The greater part of the present Abbey church was built between the years 1245 and 1269. It had been Henry III's intention to rebuild the whole church, but at his death in 1272 the building was incomplete and the nave of the Confessor's church was left linked on to the new choir. It was not until a hundred years later that the rebuilding of the nave was undertaken. By a happy inspiration the work was carried out in harmony with the style of the rest of the church, although it was not finally completed until the early years of the sixteenth century. Such conservatism is almost unique, and few, at first sight, realize that the whole of the Abbey church was not built at the same time.

The rebuilding of the eastern part of the church under Henry III was completed in two stages. During the first of these, from 1245 to 1255, Master Henry was in charge of the work. To this period belong the whole of the east end as far as one bay west of the central crossing, the apsidal chapels, the transepts and north front, St Faith's chapel, the chapter house and part of the east cloister. To Master Henry, therefore, as Lethaby pointed out, is due the whole of the planning of the church and 'everything most characteristic of Westminster.'[5] It was not an easy task, for apart from everything else he was limited by the fact that the ground plan was already laid down by the Confessor's church and its monastic buildings together with the new Lady Chapel at the east end, and by the necessity of disturbing the daily life of the monks as little as might be during the rebuilding. But he triumphed over difficulties and stamped his individuality on the church in many ways. He gave it a height exceeded by no medieval cathedral in England; he placed his choir west of the central crossing, thus retaining a feature of the Confessor's church, and by so doing giving a central space (as at Reims) under the lantern wherein takes place the main part of the coronation service; moreover, he lengthened his transepts and built a polygonal chapter house which is a marvel of grace and beauty. Both the last features are distinctively English and have no parallel in France.

Master Henry seems to have died about 1253 and was succeeded as the king's master mason by John of Gloucester. Judging from the Abbey archives and other indications he does not seem to have been much at Westminster, and for the next few years and until his death in 1260–61 little seems to have been done beyond perfecting what was already substantially completed and preparing for further work. With the appointment of Robert of Beverley as his successor there opened the second stage of activity which continued until the dedication of the church, complete except for the nave, in 1269. To this period, therefore, belongs the building of the choir and the first bay to the west of the choir screen. The new master mason, as his name implies, must have been familiar with the new Minster church at Beverley and there are echoes of Beverley at Westminster. There is, in fact, little trace of foreign influence in his work at Westminster.

To this period belongs the superb series of carved and painted shields in the spandrels of the wall arcade of the choir aisles (Pl. 29). They bear the arms of those barons and others who are said by tradition to have contributed to the cost of the church. Among them is the ramping lion of the de Montforts, and this must surely have been in place before 1264, when Simon de Montfort was in open revolt against the king.[6] These painted shields, which are magnificent examples of early heraldry, are also evidence of the colour which was used so profusely in the original decoration of the church. This colouring is the one feature of Henry's church which has largely disappeared. Much has been done of recent years in various ways, such as by cleaning and polishing the Purbeck pillars, by sumptuous fittings – altar frontals, banners, and so forth – to repair the deficiency, but at best it can be but a pale reflection of the brilliant and possibly rather overwhelming effect which the interior of the church must once have presented. There is not the slightest doubt – and it is becoming more apparent as systematic cleaning progresses – that, apart from actual wall paintings, not only were walls whitened and divided into a kind of brick pattern with red lines and roses in the centre, but bosses, vaulting ribs, sculptures, and the carvings of the spandrels of wall arcades were either gilded or painted with bright colours. On many of these traces of colour still remain.[7] In 1936, for instance, cleaning revealed that in St Benedict's Chapel part of the wall had been painted with fleurs-de-lys on a red ground, while the capitals of the wall arcade had been copper-green, the roll-mouldings had been red, and the arcade spandrels had a pattern of green leaves and red berries. When we add to all this the colour from the original windows, the polished Purbeck pillars and the great mosaic pavement in front of the High Altar, together with the magnificence of the shrine of the Confessor and the royal and other tombs with their gilt or painted effigies and heraldry[8], we can get some idea of what the interior of the church must once have looked like. There is this further point to be considered. Until a few years ago we were accustomed to think of the interior of the Abbey as being somewhat subdued and even sombre in colouring. This was partly due to the rather unfortunate and unforeseen darkening which resulted from the shellac preservative with which Sir Gilbert Scott had indurated the walls about eighty years ago and partly to the accumulated dirt of centuries. No one who has not seen it can realize the extent to which the delicate sculpture and mouldings of the north transept, for instance, are encrusted with thick layers of grime. When in 1930 a great scheme of cleaning was initiated and, as a result, the south transept was seen cleaned from floor to vaulting – followed by part of the apse to the triforium level, and Henry VII's Chapel – the whiteness of the stone beneath came almost as a revelation, and it was an endless delight to watch the details emerging sharp and clear and freed from the dirt which had blurred them.

The south transept, as has been said, dates from 1245 to 1253, and it is worth while considering in some detail its south or end wall with its great rose-window (Pl. 5). It is a work masterly alike in its conception and in its execution. It contains some of the supreme things within the Abbey church, and it is, indeed, so lovely, especially on a summer evening when the whole transept is filled with sunshine, that it can be studied and restudied in all its details and with ever increasing delight. It is divided into five stages. The lowest stage consists of five bays of which four are occupied by a wall arcade. The spandrels above this arcade have diaper work and the mouldings of the arches are enriched with carved (and once brightly-coloured) roses (Pl. 39), representations of which are so marked a feature of the decoration of the church.[9] The fifth or westernmost bay is now blocked and is masked by Roubiliac's monument to the Duke of Argyll. This bay is slightly higher than the others and through it descended originally the night-stairs from the Monks' Dorter. Until 1936 the two easternmost bays were largely obscured by two eighteenth-century monuments. Upon their removal, to facilitate the cleaning scheme, faint traces of colour were found on the dun-coloured wall behind them. With infinite care the shellac preservative and the dirt beneath it were removed and gradually there emerged two great wall-paintings (Pl. 37–39). The discovery was the more remarkable inasmuch as their existence was completely unsuspected and no record of any paintings on this wall had survived. The subjects represented are those of the legend of St Christopher and the Incredulity of St Thomas. In the opinion of Professor Tristram these great figures – they are some nine feet high – 'must rank amongst the most important survivals of wall painting ... in the whole of England'.[10] St Christopher, who bears the Christ-child on his shoulder, is painted in oil colour on a green background formerly diapered with small rosettes. He carries

12

a staff and wears a robe of lake colour, while the Child is clothed in a light tunic and carries an apple in his right hand. On the wall is a partly-mutilated inscription relating to St Christopher. The rather unusual subject of the Incredulity of St Thomas is painted on a vivid vermilion ground diapered with golden fleurs-de-lys. Our Lord wears a mantle of lake colour, while St Thomas, in a pale yellow tunic with a dark green mantle, kneels and thrusts his hand into Our Lord's side. Further traces of colour elsewhere suggest that these paintings were probably two of a series of which the others have totally perished. 'The dignity of their conception' – to quote Professor Tristram again – 'their beauty of colour, and their technical handling indicate the hand of a master.' They date probably from about 1280 to 1300, and it is not unlikely that they were painted by Master Walter of Durham, traces of whose painting remain on the Coronation Chair and on the base of the tomb of Queen Eleanor.

The second stage (Pl. 5) above these paintings contains the wall passage which runs round the church at this level. A few years ago some slight traces of red colour painted on parchment were found on the back wall. This was probably all that remained of a further series of wall paintings otherwise completely destroyed, which had had verses painted on parchment beneath them. There are similar parchment slips under paintings still existing in the chapter house.

The third stage at its base carries on the line of the capitals of the piers of the transept. It extends upwards to the level, and continues the line, of the string course of the triforium. It contains six deeply set windows with trefoiled heads contrasting with the lancets of the similar stage in the north transept. The triple-shafted splays of these windows with their moulded capitals and bases are singularly beautiful. These recessed windows form the central feature of the whole composition and accentuate its perfect proportions.

The fourth stage continues the arcade of the triforium, but here, in glorious contrast to the beautiful austerity of the stage below, the carver and the sculptor have been given full scope (Pl. 13, 14, 25–28). In contrast also to the corresponding stage in the north transept, the wall at the back has been pierced for windows. The three arches of this stage are uniform with the rest of those in the triforium but, as elsewhere, they are enlivened by slightly differing decoration. The westernmost bay has the outer order of its arches enriched by diaper work, the middle bay has simple trefoil foliage, while the easternmost bay is perfectly plain except at the intersection with its neighbour, where a sprig of foliage charmingly curves and strays over the mouldings. At the apex of the middle arch is a little carved head of a mitred Abbot – Richard de Berking or Richard de Crokesley – who thus unobtrusively and delightfully marks his connexion with this part of the building (Pl. 32).

In the diapered spandrels of this stage are the four great figures representing (almost certainly) Edward the Confessor giving his ring to the Pilgrim (who subsequently revealed himself to be St John) with two attendant censing angels (Pl. 25). The central figure to the east represents the king standing on a crouching figure. He is now headless, but cleaning revealed that he is wearing a cream-coloured tunic, a gold mantle lined with green, red hose, and black shoes. The other central figure is larger and represents a seated figure with bare feet and wearing a pilgrim's hat. His right arm is fully extended as if to receive the ring and the hand rests on a projecting stone of carved foliage. His left hand supported a staff. His tunic is also cream-coloured, and his mantle, lined with vermilion, is caught up in a knot on the right shoulder. Both these figures are much weathered and are of a different stone from the angels in the spandrels.

These two angels are the supreme examples of thir-teenth-century art within the Abbey church, masterly in their conception and perfect in their poise and grace (Pl. 26–28). They are, perhaps, the loveliest things of their kind in England, and are equal to anything to be found in France. They are indeed 'the very embodiment of rapture'[11]; the one to the west pensively serious, the other to the east, even more enchanting, graciously smil-ing like the more famous angel at Reims. When in 1930 it was possible to examine them closely from a staging erected across the south transept, it was found that their wings had been picked out with gold, green, red and black, and that their vestments had been brightly coloured and patterned with red and black spots and with little red crosses with green spots at their extremities. They are probably the work of Master John of St. Albans, 'sculptor of the king's images' and his school of assistants, whose hands may also, perhaps, be seen in the scarcely less lovely figures representing the Annunciation in the chapter house. Lethaby made the very interesting suggestion that, as the slightly later angels in the Angel Choir at Lincoln have a marked affinity with our angels, it was not unlikely that the Westminster sculptors went on to Lincoln, where, indeed, there are many features which seem to derive from Westminster.[12]

Certainly all these angels have that quality of serenity which, as Mâle has pointed out, the sculptors of the thirteenth century were able to reproduce for a few brief years when medieval art reached its climax; for, as a recent French writer on angel-sculpture has said 'Ils sont réels, graves, mais souriants. Dans leur sourire perce parfois un peu de malice, ils sont si fins, ils comprennent si vite tant de belles et grandes choses. Mais bien plus que la joie, c'est le bonheur complet et profond qui rayonne sur leur figure. Ces figures de pierre sont comme illuminées par le sourire, et plus encore par la sérénité, la paix de ce front si limpide, de ces yeux qui voient si loin, qui sont si largement et si paisiblement ouverts sur l'invisible, qui, sans effort, d'un seul regard embrassent tout, puis qu'ils voient Dieu.'[13]

The fifth stage is filled by the great rose-window which rises to the full height of the vault. The stonework of the rose is modern and so is the not unpleasing glass with which both it and the windows in the stages below are filled.[14] It is, however, important to notice that through successive restorations the form of the original thirteenth-century rose has almost certainly been preserved. It exactly corresponds to the representation of a rose-window which is found on the contemporary tiles of the chapter house. These great rose-windows framed in squares and with the bottom spandrels pierced, thus subtly connecting them with the windows beneath, were essentially French and were the glory of the thirteenth-century cathedrals in northern France.[15] The south transept rose and that of the north transept (though the details of the original form of the latter have disappeared in successive restorations) are unique in England. Nothing shows more clearly how fascinated the Westminster master mason must have been by what he had seen and studied abroad and how he must have determined that Westminster too should have its rose-windows which should not only be comparable to, but even outshine, the noblest examples in France.

We have dwelt on the details of this south transept wall, because perhaps nowhere else is the beauty, and what an Elizabethan writer called the 'lightsomeness', of this great church so concentrated. Its setting is accentuated by the unusual length of the transept as compared with those of contemporary French cathedrals. The vivid colouring of the wall-paintings below leads up to the brilliance of the painted glass above, with the cool grey-green polished shafts of the Purbeck pillars of the arcades so subtly disposed that the straight upward sweep of their lines inevitably leads the eye to the glorious rose and the lines of the vaulting above. One begins then to see that 'the half has not been told' of what this great Abbey church has to unfold to those who can lift their eyes above the monuments – though, let us add, those sometimes much-abused monuments are very much a part of the Abbey to those who know them best.

The interior of the north transept with its rose-window corresponds in essentials with that of the south transept. It seems a few years later in date, owing, perhaps, to the time spent on the building of the original exterior façade. The two principal figures under the rose have disappeared and no record remains of what they represented. The angels, however, with their censers remain in the spandrels. They are graver than those in the south transept, and lack something of their poise and grace, but none the less they are very noble and beautiful figures. It must be remembered, too, that they – and all this transept – have yet to be cleaned and are encrusted with dust and grime. The middle spandrels of this stage are enriched by exceptionally beautiful carved stiff-leaf foliage, and this reappears, though mutilated, on the lowest or ground floor stage both of the centre wall and also in the aisles to the transept.[16] Almost completely hidden on the soffits of the lancet windows of the third stage are panels containing twenty-four half-figures of angels, of great delicacy and charm, playing various instruments of music (Pl. 30). Immediately over the centre column of the main door, at the intersection of the arches, is a remarkable head representing a youthful king or prince and carved with great care and character – perhaps from its special position meant to represent Henry III's son, the future Edward I (Pl. 15) – while high up under the corbel of one of the missing figures beneath the rose is a no less remarkable head, also full of character, which seems to be intended for a master mason (Pl. 14). One would like to believe that it represents John of Gloucester or Robert of Beverley. Such heads of master masons are not uncommon. There are noteworthy examples of slightly later date, for instance, in the choir at Exeter and in the chapter house at Southwell. But these heads, interesting as they may be in themselves, are, in a sense, merely part of the ordinary decoration of all great churches. More interesting, because they are so characteristic of the medieval carver, are the heads and other carvings which, as Mâle put it in a picturesque phrase, ' seules apercevaient les hirondelles. Ce qui ne se voit pas est aussi parfait que ce qui se voit. L'art fleurit partout avec une prodigalité, une indifférence pour l'admiration, qui font penser aux œuvres de la nature.'[17]

Among such carvings are a series of large corbel heads at the east end of the triforium, in that vast upper Abbey church reproducing the ground plan of the aisles and chapels below, which the ordinary visitor hardly ever sees and of which the original purpose has never been satisfactorily explained. These heads – there are seventeen of them – date from the building of the church and are carved with immense vigour and enjoyment. Some of them are obvious caricatures, perhaps of some of the craftsmen engaged on the building (Pl. 17), while one is of such outstanding beauty and thoughtfulness that it may claim to be one of the supreme things within the Abbey church (Pl. 16). This noble and lovely head has that curious suggestion of Greek fifth-century art which, as has been noted more than once, distinguishes some of

the best of thirteenth-century sculpture.[18] A pleasant
fancy has christened it 'Master Henry '. It is, indeed, thus
that one would wish to think of the man who conceived
and built this portion of the church, although, in fact,
it is probably nothing more than yet another example of
that curious strain in the medieval craftsman which in-
duced him to mingle indifferently grave with gay, horror
and suffering with beauty and serenity. Such representations of suffering seem for the most part to be confined,
at any rate in the thirteenth century, to representations
of ordinary mortals and range from the trivial ills of life
to horrible carvings on bosses and elsewhere of human
beings in process of being devoured by animals (Pl. 19).
We meet with it again still more strikingly in St Faith's
Chapel where there are some large and remarkable heads
on corbels which carry the springers of the vault. They
also are mid-thirteenth century and have recently been
cleaned. They include a head of negroid type of a sinister
evilness and power not paralleled elsewhere in the Abbey
(Pl. 35), together with a head of lovely serenity and
beauty known as 'the dreaming youth' (Pl. 33). Here,
too, are gracious and smiling ladies in juxtaposition with
heads distorted by pain. These latter have such a marked
individuality with their open mouths and prominent teeth
that they are probably the work of the same carver. A
head of much the same type, which was recently found at
Henry III's palace at Clarendon, may well be from the
same hand.

Above the altar in this chapel is a striking painting,
dating from the second half of the thirteenth century, of

St Faith, a tall crowned figure, under a canopy, dressed in a purple robe and holding a book and a gridiron. Beneath is a little painting of the Crucifixion, while on the wall at the side is painted the kneeling figure of a Benedictine monk who directs a prayer towards the Saint. If, as seems probable, this represents William, a monk of Westminster, 'our beloved painter' as Henry III called him, it is one of the very few instances where a monk personally contributed to the decoration of an Abbey church. William was a contemporary of Walter of Durham who in 1300–1 was engaged upon the decoration of the Coronation Chair (Pl. 42–43). The chair itself, which was made to contain the Stone of Scone, is of oak and has been much mutilated. Little remains of the gilt gesso decoration on the inside face of the chair which portrayed a king seated on a throne with a lion at his feet, but on the inside of the arms are little diapered panels containing foliage and grotesques and a delightful design of birds and oak leaves. The outside panels also have foliage decoration. The seat of the chair is made to slide out and disclose the Stone of Scone beneath.

Of about the same date, or perhaps a little later, are the full-length painted figures on the Sedilia by the High Altar (Pl. 44). They are about eight feet high and are painted with great distinction. On the side towards the ambulatory is the Confessor with crown and sceptre, dressed in a fur-lined robe and holding up his ring. He was probably giving it to St John as a Pilgrim although this figure has entirely disappeared from the adjoining panel. In the other two panels are the remains of an Annunciation. On

the altar side are two kings who have not been satisfactorily identified although it is reasonable to suppose
that they represent founders of the church. They both
have furred robes and carry sceptres and the background
of the younger one is powdered with leopards. The two
other panels on this side have been totally obliterated – no
doubt by Thomas Gassaway and his companions, when in
1644 they were employed in 'raffing out the painted
images' in the Church. On the pendants of the truncated
pinnacles between the arches are very attractive painted
woodcarvings. They represent two young crowned heads
and an Abbot who is possibly Walter de Wenlock (1283–
1307 (Pl. 45).

Two other paintings of later date – apart from those in
the chapter house and the celebrated portrait of Richard
II – may also be mentioned. About 1376 the interesting
little Chapel of Our Lady of the Pew was constructed in
the thickness of the wall between the Chapel of St John
the Baptist and that of Abbot Islip. It was endowed by
Mary de Sancto Paulo as a chantry chapel for the soul of
her husband, Aymer de Valence, Earl of Pembroke, whose
tomb is close by. This chapel now forms the entry to
St John's Chapel, but originally it was self-contained and
was entered only from the ambulatory through wooden
half-length gates which with their original iron chevaux-
de-frise still remain (Pl. 46). Cleaning revealed that the
mouldings of the outer door are very delicately painted in
vermilion with a diapering of black lines on white. The
opposite wall contains a niche on which must have stood
an image of the Virgin. The remains of the Glory round

her head can still be seen painted on the wall. The walls of the chapel have a painted pattern of what appear to be pine-cones, and among them is a small white hart with a crown round its neck. There are also coloured bosses in the vaulting including an Assumption. This little chapel must have been very splendid, and the offerings made at it rivalled those made at the High Altar and were a substantial item in the Sacrist's annual accounts.[19]

A larger and much more imposing painting of Richard II's badge of the couched hart can be seen on the wall of the muniment room. The room forms an open gallery half-way between the floor and the triforium on the west side of the south transept (Pl. 47), and is part of the original building of 1245–53. It provides an interesting example of how Master Henry triumphed over the difficulties of the site. In order to provide a western aisle to the south transept he was forced to incorporate part of the east cloister in the church, and on the roof of it he constructed the muniment room open on two sides, giving to it at its south end a window of three graduated lancets corresponding to a similar window in the west aisle of the north transept. He thus got exactly the effect he wanted. The muniment room, besides its later fittings, which include some early muniment chests and cupboards and a complete fourteenth-century pavement of slip-tiles, has some very charming corbel heads together with some foliated capitals to the windows (Pl. 8–9). One of these capitals – and it is unique in the Abbey – has a couple of hawks among the foliage which curls over very delightfully on to the wall beyond. These foliated capitals, both here and elsewhere and in the wall arcades, are characteristic of the earliest stage of the rebuilding under Master Henry. They do not appear in the later thirteenth-century work, in which the builders were contented with moulded capitals, partly no doubt owing to the difficulty of carving the rather stubborn Purbeck marble. The foliated capitals follow the usual English types of the period, both stiff-leaved and naturalistic, though Sir Gilbert Scott thought that he could detect the work of one French carver in some of the capitals of the wall arcades.[20] 'Many of these,' he wrote, 'are of the English type of the period, but among them are two kinds, both of which are in their carving distinctly French. The one is the crocket capital, the stalks of which are terminated, not as in English work with conventional, but with exquisite little tufts of natural foliage, such as may be seen in the wall arcading of the Sainte Chapelle, and many other French works of the period. In the other, natural foliage is introduced creeping up the bell, and turning over at the top in symmetrical tufts. In both the foliage is smaller and less bold than in French work, and the architectural form of the capital is English.'[21] These 'French' capitals appear again in the Poets' Corner and west cloister doorways.

To return to the muniment room. In the vault of the window recess at the south end (Pl. 24) are three very remarkable bosses which have retained their original colouring and represent combats between centaurs, dragons and angels (Pl. 22–23). The main vault of the muniment room, as well as the vaults of the aisles of the transepts, have large figure-subject bosses. Some of them are obscured by dirt and have been mutilated, but among them are a very beautiful Annunciation (Pl. 21), a Coronation of the Virgin, and Two Souls in Abraham's Bosom. Other subjects include King David with a harp (Pl. 20), a cock among foliage, and lions rending a man. All these bosses date from the thirteenth century, and so do those of the main vault of the apse and choir which represent various types of foliage (Pl. 18). The bosses in the nave and its aisles have mainly foliage and heraldic subjects and show a gradual deterioration as the work of rebuilding in the fifteenth and early sixteenth centuries proceeded.

During the first half of the fifteenth century the chantry chapel and tomb of Henry V was erected at the east end of the Confessor's Chapel under the direction of John Thirsk, the master mason then in charge of the rebuilding of the nave. It consists of the tomb itself, with a chantry chapel above extending over the ambulatory. This chapel is reached by two octagonal stair-turrets with open-work stone tracery. The idea seems to have been derived from the stair-turrets leading to the relic tribune at the Sainte Chapelle. These turrets are embellished with large sculptured figures of kings and saints. Prominent among them are Edward the Confessor in royal robes and St John as a pilgrim. They occupy pedestals over the south and north turret doors respectively. Although somewhat weathered they are dignified and impressive figures. Over the reredos in the chantry chapel above is a further fine series representing from north to south St George, St Edmund as a king, the angel Gabriel, an empty niche which possibly once had a representation of the Trinity, the Virgin,

Edward the Confessor, and St Denis (the patron saint of France) carrying his head. The presence of these two patron saints refers to the fact that by the Treaty of Troyes Henry V was to succeed eventually to the throne of France as well as to that of England (Pl. 49). The outer faces of the bridge over the ambulatory are of considerable interest, for they contain sculptured scenes from contemporary history. On the north side in the centre is the Coronation of Henry V with the Archbishop placing the crown on the king's head. The corresponding scene on the south side represents the Homage ceremony. The niches on each side of these scenes contain fifty-three little figures of peers, judges, bishops, and so on, assisting at the ceremony in their appropriate robes – incidentally the earliest representation of these robes with the distinctive attributes of the rank of the wearers. On the return side walls are two representations of the king in armour and mounted upon a charger in full career (Pl. 48). They are very spirited and delightful. On the oak beam above the chantry chapel hang the shield, helm, and saddle which were carried at Henry's funeral and are probably part of 'the whole armour of a man' which after the funeral became the property of the church. The oak shield formerly bore the king's arms, but of these no trace remains. On the back is a covering of blue silk powdered with fleurs-de-lys and on the arm band are the arms of Navarre (a cross saltire and double orle of chains) apparently those of Joan of Navarre, second wife of Henry IV. The helm is a genuine tilting helm and once carried a crest. The saddle is of wood with a padded seat and is the only one of its kind in existence in England.

The cornices of the chapel are enriched by the king's badges – chained swans, antelopes, and lighted beacons – and the vault above the ambulatory has more Bohun swans and antelopes couched and with twisted napkins about their necks. In the chantry chapel above are little trefoils which contain irradiated figures of Our Lady and Child with her moon attribute beneath, and of the maiden with the unicorn.[22] The form of these trefoils is exactly repeated on the stone screen between the Sanctuary and the Confessor's Chapel which was also the work of John Thirsk. It was finally completed in 1441.[23] It is not always realised how this screen breaks the circle of royal tombs which really extend to the steps of the High Altar. Before its erection it would have been obvious that the tomb of Edward I was next to that of his brother Edmund Crouchback from which it is now completely cut off. The screen remains unrestored on the chapel side, though it has been much defaced. It must originally have been a most elaborate affair with canopied and painted niches filled with saints. In the cornice are fourteen little carved scenes from the life of Edward the Confessor (Pl. 50–51).[24]

The western side of the screen has been entirely restored although we know that originally it had a recess for a retable above the altar. The original painted retable, dating from the second half of the thirteenth century, still exists, though in a sadly mutilated condition, and stands in the south ambulatory (Pl. 40-41). It is of oak, rectangular in shape (about 11 by 3 ft.) with elaborate gesso and coloured glass decoration. Its provenance is disputed, but it seems probable that it is English rather than French work. 'In many respects it stands absolutely alone in Europe, combining as it does all the delicacy and minuteness of the finest miniature with the more solid technique and greater depth and luminosity of oil painting.'[25] In the centre under canopies are painted standing figures of Our Lord and (perhaps) the Virgin and St John. The globe carried by Our Lord is a miracle of minute painting. Although little more than an inch in diameter it depicts the Universe, represented by water with a boat upon it, land with trees, sheep and a stork, and sky with sun, moon, clouds and birds. To the left of the central compartments are four little panels with paintings of miracles; the three which remain depict the healing of Jairus's daughter, the feeding of the five thousand, and the healing of the blind man. At the end, also under a canopy, is a very beautiful painting of St Peter. The other side is completely defaced, but we know that at the end was a figure of St Paul corresponding to that of St Peter. This unique example of thirteenth-century art has had a remarkable history. For some reason it escaped destruction in the sixteenth century and must have lain about until in 1606 it was used by the Abbey carpenter as a bit of old board to form the roof of 'the presse of wainscott' which he was making in the Islip Chapel to contain the wax and wooden effigies. There it remained for over two hundred years unknown except to a few antiquaries in the eighteenth century who noted the existence of some curious painting in this position. This, however, did not save it from having the whole of one side deliberately defaced when the wax effigy of Chatham was placed beneath it in 1779. It was finally rescued by Edward Blore, the Abbey Surveyor, in 1827, and since then has been one of the major treasures of the Abbey.[26]

The chantry chapel of Abbot Islip (1500–32) in the north ambulatory, where the retable remained for so many years, was erected during the Abbot's lifetime, for it is depicted in his Mortuary Roll which is preserved among the Abbey muniments and contains the only known pre-Reformation drawings of the Abbey church. The chapel is in two storeys, the front to the ambulatory having the lower part filled by the door and by two open traceried windows through which can be seen the chapel in which the Abbot is buried; the upper storey has seven canopied but now empty niches. In the cornice between the two storeys are the Abbot's coat of arms and his rebus – a human eye and a slip of a tree grasped by a hand, and a tree with a man slipping from it (Pl. 64). In the chapel above are monochrome paintings of St Peter and Edward the Confessor under canopies.

In the muniment room is preserved a most remarkable carved stone head of an Abbot in a richly jewelled mitre with lappets (Pl. 63). The nose is slightly broken and the front of the mitre has lost its surface. The head is superbly carved, and the expression is one of great dignity and compassion though not without a touch of sternness about the mouth. It dates from the early years of the sixteenth century and almost certainly is a portrait of Abbot Islip, the greatest of the later Abbots. There are some puzzling features about it. There is no very obvious place in the

Abbey from which it might have come. It is of a different stone from any of the figures in Henry VII's Chapel, and from the set of the head it is difficult to believe that it could ever have belonged to a figure standing erect in a niche. On the other hand, from the marked droop of the eyelids it was evidently meant to be seen from below. But whatever its provenance its actual history is not the least remarkable thing about it. About 1887 it was 'found in the core of the north-east buttress of the north transept' where it had evidently been put as a bit of old stone filling by one of the workmen of Sir Christopher Wren who repaired that part of the north front in the early eighteenth century. It subsequently lay about with other carved stones and it was only recently that the great beauty of the head and the artistic quality of its carving were recognized.[27]

Abbot Islip was present and assisted at the laying of the foundation stone in 1503 of Henry VII's new chapel which replaced the original thirteenth-century Lady Chapel. The great work of rebuilding the nave was then nearing completion, and the building of the new Lady Chapel was the last considerable medieval addition to the fabric. The chapel, which has come to be identified with the king who first planned it and whose tomb and chantry chapel form the principal object within it, was almost certainly designed by Robert Vertue. He and his brother William were the outstanding master masons of the time. They were probably recommended for the work by Sir Reginald Bray who took a deep interest in the building. Among the Abbey muniments is a letter written to him about this time by Bishop King of Bath in which he says: 'Robert and William Vertu have been here with me that can make unto you Rapport of the state and forwardenes of this oure chirche of bathe. And also of the Vawte devised for the chancelle of the said chirche. Wherunto as they say nowe ther shal be noone so goodely neither in england nor in france. And thereof they make theym fast and sure.'[28] No one will deny the beauty of the vaulting at Bath Abbey, but at Westminster the Vertues were to erect a vault which was even more 'goodely' and has never failed to enchant and fascinate by the skill and daring of its construction (Pl. 52-57). It was the more striking inasmuch as, owing to the conservatism of Yevele and his successors, who were rightly content in vaulting the nave to copy their thirteenth-century predecessors, Westminster had no such elaborate lierne vault as may be seen, for instance, at Norwich, Winchester or Gloucester, and in that sense was out of touch with the architecture of the age.

For some time the medieval masons had been feeling their way gradually to a new development of these ribbed or lierne vaults. The result was a kind of inverted cone decorated with ribs or, as it is usually called, fan-vaulting of which the first example was the cloister at Gloucester (1351–77). Further examples may be seen at Sherborne Abbey (1490) and at King's College, Cambridge (1512–15). But these vaults, beautiful as they are, tend to become monotonous, and a yet more daring innovation was made which was to culminate in the marvel of the Westminster vault. This development can be traced through

31

the Divinity School at Oxford (c. 1445–80) and the slightly later Oxford cathedral choir (1478–1503), where for the first time pendants were used in combination with the lierne vault, and transverse stone arches were introduced. These arches are really the counterpart of modern steel girders while the pendants are elongated voussoirs of the arches which hold them in place. It was thus that the problem of vaulting over a wide space with fan-tracery was solved.[29] The vault of Henry VII's Chapel is based on that of the Oxford Divinity School with certain improvements and modifications. It depends again, as at Oxford, on great transverse arches (with a 33-ft. span) which spring from below the vaulting and are kept in place by outside flying buttresses. But at Westminster these arches pass right through the vault, so that instead of being visible throughout as at Oxford the crown of the arch is invisible from below. They are made up of wedge-shaped stones or voussoirs and each of the great pendants is merely one of these voussoirs elongated to a solid length of about eight feet. Thus having got the pendants firmly wedged in the arch they can be safely built up as a cone-shaped fan while the smaller pendants in the vault are, as it were, dropped in from above and bind the whole together. The result is a vault which is one of the most astonishing ever contrived by man and as ingenious as it is simple.

When it was thoroughly cleaned, examined and repaired in 1933 and more recently, it was found to have no structural defects – apart from the fact that some of the stones in the pockets had slipped and that some of the joints were defective – and only the purely ornamental carved cusps on the arches which were added by the builders when the vault was completed, were at all in a dangerous state.

The splendour of the vault was, however, only part of the magnificence of the chapel which Lethaby has called 'one of the most perfect buildings ever erected in England'. The original intention had been that the king's tomb within its 'grate, in maner of a Closure, of coper and gilte' should occupy the middle of the chapel where it would immediately face those entering through the great gilt bronze and oak gates at the west end of the chapel. It would thus have been seen in relation to the chapel as a whole and to the stalls with their elaborate woodwork and carved misericords, which are, indeed, set well back – almost cramped – to allow space for the tomb. Beyond was to have been the tomb of Henry VI surrounded by further royal tombs in the radiating chapels and in the aisles. But, eventually, Henry VI was buried elsewhere, and Henry VII's tomb was placed further to the east in its present position behind the altar. The result was that the proportions of the chapel were somewhat marred. In all other respects, however, the wishes of the founder were carried out. The great clerestory windows were filled with painted glass of such magnificence that Barnard Flower, the king's glazier, was instructed to take them as his pattern for the windows of the Chapel of King's College, Cambridge; the triforium storey below was so contrived that it consists of elaborately canopied niches containing a unique collection of statues of saints;

while the walls, doors, windows, arches and vaults were 'garnished and adorned with our arms, badges, and cognisants ... in as goodly and rich manner as such work requireth.' Some of the king's beasts – lions, dragons, greyhounds – which are placed on the capitals of the piers in the vestibule and more especially those in the side aisles, where they have been sheltered and almost hidden behind the springing of the vaulting, are most engaging little animals (Pl. 58–59). Rather larger representations of the same beasts look down from the tops of the canopies over the saints in the radiating and side chapels.

The painted windows, which were deliberately destroyed in 1643–4, almost certainly 'contained the Gospel story with parallels from the Old Testament, together with messengers of bigger scale in each window, except that the east window would have had the Crucifixion only'.[30] In the windows of the chapels were badges and coats of arms, and some of these were destroyed by blast from bombs in the recent war. The sculptured saints in the triforium also follow a definite scheme, the figure of Christ at the east end is surrounded by Apostles and saints as assessors of the Last Judgment. These saints, as those who saw them when they were on exhibition at the Victoria and Albert Museum in 1945 will remember, are full of character, vigour, and humour, and form a series unrivalled in England. Originally they numbered 107, and of these nearly a hundred remain. They are the work of several carvers of varying merit, and some may even have come from the earlier Lady Chapel. Among the most striking are the delightful St Anne teaching the Virgin to read (Pl. 61), St Matthew, with spectacles on nose, using the head of an angel as a writing desk (Pl. 60), the martyrdom of St Sebastian, St Wilgefortis with the beard which was sent to her in answer to her prayers that she might be protected from the snare of beauty (Pl. 62), and St Jerome wearing his Cardinal's hat and accompanied by his lion (Pl. 62). It is well to remember that all these saints should be seen in their setting as part of a definite scheme 'redily devised' by the king himself, and no king has a more splendid mausoleum. Perhaps we may sum it up in the words of a foreigner who saw the chapel some seventy years after its completion and wrote of it as 'a very fair sight and of marvellous workmanship, and one cannot see nor speak of anything fairer, be it for the work within or without this Chapel ... nor do I think that anywhere in the world can the like be seen, nor one so fairly adorned'.[31]

It is a remarkable fact that when at length the Chapel was completed and the agelong story of medieval building and rebuilding at Westminster was thus at last brought to a close, less than twenty years were to elapse before the whole Abbey church was grievously mutilated and denuded of the greater part of the splendour of its interior fittings by the dissolution of the monastery in 1540. But although much was taken much also remained, and we cannot but be thankful that this great church has continued down the centuries as a place of worship and consecration, and that it was spared almost unharmed in the hour of its greatest danger, to remain serene and incomparable, alike in its beauty and in the majesty of its associations.

1. See A.W.Clapham, *Romanesque Architecture in Western Europe* (1936), pp.139–41, and L.E.Tanner and A.W.Clapham, *Recent Excavations in the Nave of Westminster Abbey* (*Archæologia*, Vol. LXXXIII, 1933).

2. Emile Mâle, *L'Art allemand et l'art français*, 1923, p.181.

3. W.R.Lethaby, *Westminster Abbey and The King's Craftsmen*, 1906, p.125, and *Westminster Abbey Re-Examined*, 1925, p.86.

4. Lethaby, *Re-Examined*, pp.46 et seq.

5. Lethaby, *Re-Examined*, pp.43–44.

6. The existing shields are as follows: (South Aisle of Choir, East to West) (1) Edward the Confessor, (2) England, (3) Provence, (4) Quincy, (5) Lacy, (6) Earl of Cornwall, (7) Ross. (North Aisle of Choir, East to West) (1) The Empire, (2) France, (3) Clare, (4) Bigod, (5) Montfort, (6) Warenne, (7) Forz.

7. Curiously enough, when the south transept was cleaned no trace of colour was found on the diaper of the spandrels of the main arches, although Sir Gilbert Scott had noted that they had once been gilt on a red ground.

8. A King Penguin Book dealing entirely with the royal tombs in Westminster Abbey is in preparation.

9. Lethaby, *Craftsmen*, pp.49 et seq.

10. See *Burlington Magazine*, May 1937.

11. Lethaby, *Re-Examined*, p.185.

12. Lethaby, *Re-Examined*, p.188.

13. See Professor Joseph Duhr, s.j., in *Dictionnaire de spiritualité ascétique et mystique*, 1937, Vol. 1, pp. 619 et seq. I am indebted for this reference to the Rev. J. Brodrick, s.j.

14. The window was restored and the present glass put in as a memorial to Hugh, 1st Duke of Westminster, in 1902.

15. Lethaby, *Craftsmen*, pp.72–75 and 135.

16. It has often been pointed out that Stone Church, near Dartford, Kent, bears a remarkable resemblance to the Abbey, and it has been suggested that it was built by the Abbey masons. The carvings in the spandrels of the wall-arcade round the chancel at Stone closely resemble the carvings in the spandrels of the north transept at West-

minster. See A. Gardner, *English Gothic Foliage Sculpture*, 1927, pp. 26–27 and Plates 38–39.

17. Mâle, *Art et artistes du moyen âge*, 1927, p. 229.

18. See A. Gardner, *English Medieval Sculpture*, 1935, p. 130.

19. This Chapel has only been identified of recent years. It was formerly erroneously called the Chapel of St Erasmus or Little St Mary. 'Pew' in this sense seems to mean a small enclosed space or private oratory. There was a similar chapel within the Palace of Westminster. See C. L. Kingsford, 'Our Lady of the Pew. The King's Oratory or Closet in the Palace of Westminster' (*Archæologia*, Vol. LXVIII, 1917).

20. G. Gilbert Scott, *Gleanings from Westminster Abbey*, 1863, pp. 21, 32.

21. Scott, *Gleanings*, pp. 32–33.

22. See W. H. St J. Hope, 'The Funeral, Monument, and Chantry Chapel of King Henry the Fifth' (*Archæologia*, Vol. LXV, 1914).

23. The Screen is usually said to be mid-fifteenth century. An entry, however, in the Sacrist's Account Roll for 1441 (W.A.M. 19693) shows that it was completed in that year, for, by the order of the Abbot, xxs. was given to John Thrysk and others 'pro posicione ultimi lapidis super le Reredos' at the newly made High Altar.

24. The subjects depicted on the Screen are: (1) The oath of fealty, (2) The birth of the Confessor, (3) His Coronation, (4) The vision of the Devil on the Dane-gelt, (5) The thief robbing the Confessor, (6) The vision of Our Lord at Mass, (7) The drowning of the King of Denmark (Plate 50), (8) The quarrel between Harold and Tostig, (9) The vision of the Seven Sleepers of Ephesus, (10) The Confessor giving the ring to the beggar (St John), (11) The cure of the blind men, (12) The return of the ring by St John to the pilgrims from Ludlow, (13) The restoration of the ring to the king by the pilgrims, (14) The dedication of the Abbey (Plate 51).

25. E. W. Tristram, *English Medieval Mural Painting*. Lecture at the Royal Institution of Great Britain, Nov. 16, 1934.

26. See L. E. Tanner, 'The Retable at Westminster' (*The Times*, Aug. 20, 1931).

27. See for more detailed discussion L. E. Tanner, 'A Medieval Abbot'

in *Westminster Abbey Quarterly* (Vol. 1, No. 1, Jan. 1939).

28. Westminster Abbey Muniments, 16040.

29. In the same line of development is the vaulting of St George's Chapel, Windsor (*c.* 1500). This is interesting because there is little doubt that the Vertues and other masons who were employed at Westminster were working on it. For fan-vaulting see F. Bond, *Gothic Architecture in England*, 1905, pp. 342–49, and G. G. Scott, *Lectures on Rise and Development of Medieval Architecture*, 1879, 11, pp. 217–226.

30. Lethaby, *Re-Examined*, p. 179.

31. A. Hurault, Sieur de Maisse, *Journal of his Embassy to England, Nov.* 1597–*Jan.* 1598, tr. G. B. Harrison and R. A. Jones, 1931, pp. 32–33.

LIST OF PLATES

18. Boss, naturalistic foliage (Vine). *c.*1280. South aisle of the nave.

19. Boss, man torn by lions. Mid thirteenth century. North aisle of the nave.

20. Boss, King David. Mid thirteenth century. West aisle of the North transept.

21. Boss. Annunciation. Mid thirteenth century. North transept.

22. Boss, Combat between lion, centaur and dragon. Mid thirteenth century. Muniment Room.

23. Boss, combat between man and lion centaur. Mid thirteenth century. Muniment Room.

24. Lancets in the Muniment Room.

25. Pilgrim and censing angel under rose window. South transept.

26. Censing angel. East corner. South transept.

27. Censing angel. West corner. South transept.
(Censer and hand broken off.)

28. Censing angel. East corner. South transept.

29. Painted stone heraldic shield. (Simon de Montfort.) Mid thirteenth century. North aisle of the nave.

30. Angel choir. Mid thirteenth century. Soffit of lancet windows. North transept.

31. St Margaret emerging from dragon. Spandrel. North aisle of the nave.

32. Head of Abbot, triforium arch. South transept under rose window.

33. Corbel head. Mid thirteenth century (before and after cleaning). St Faith's Chapel. 'The Dreaming Youth'.

34. Corbel head. Mid thirteenth century. St Faith's Chapel.

35. Corbel head. Mid thirteenth century. St Faith's Chapel.

36. Corbel head. Mid thirteenth century. St Faith's Chapel.

37. Mural painting. Late thirteenth century. South transept. Detail of Incredulity of St Thomas.

38. Mural painting. Late thirteenth century. South transept. Incredulity of St Thomas.

39. Mural painting. Late thirteenth century. South transept. St Christopher.

40. Retable. Late thirteenth century. Central Panels.

41. Retable. Late thirteenth century. Detail of side panel. The Feeding of the Five Thousand.

42. Coronation Chair. Back. (Prepared for the Coronation, 1937.)

43. Coronation Chair.

44. Sedilia. c.1300.

45. Sedilia. Painted wooden head of Abbot Walter de Wenlok?

46. Chapel of Our Lady of the Pew. North ambulatory.

47. Mural painting. Late fourteenth century. Muniment Room. White Hart Badge of Richard II.

48. Henry V's Chantry Chapel. Detail showing Henry V on his charger.

49. Henry V's Chantry Chapel. Reredos. Fifteenth century.

50. Chapel of St Edward the Confessor. Stone Screen. Fifteenth century. The vision of the drowning of the King of Denmark.

51. Chapel of St Edward the Confessor. Stone Screen. Fifteenth century. The dedication of the Church.

52. Henry VII's Chapel. Apse during cleaning.

53. Henry VII's Chapel. South-East Apsidal Chapel before war damage to modern glass.

54. Henry VII's Chapel. Sunlight and Sculpture.

55. Henry VII's Chapel. Side Chapel.

56. Henry VII's Chapel. Fan Vaulting.

57. Henry VII's Chapel. Fan Vaulting. North Aisle.

58. Henry VII's Chapel. Shield Supporter in Vestibule.

59. Henry VII's Chapel. Heraldic Leopard.

60. Henry VII's Chapel. St Matthew and St Mark, photographed when removed from their niches.

61. Henry VII's Chapel. St Mary Magdalene and St Anne, photographed when removed from their niches.

62. Henry VII's Chapel. St Wilgefortis (Uncumber) and St Jerome, photographed when removed from their niches.

63. Stone Head of an Abbot (Abbot Islip?), early sixteenth century, in the Muniment Room.

64. Carved Rebus of Abbot Islip. Islip Chantry Chapel. Early sixteenth century. An eye and a slip. A boy slipping from a tree.

1. Towers and flying buttresses from the South.

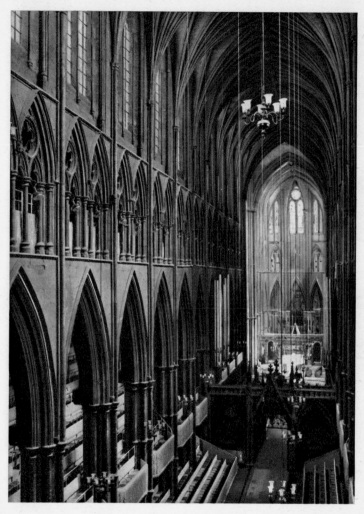

2. Nave looking East, as prepared for the Coronation 1937.

3. Choir and nave looking West.

4. The sanctuary from the Muniment Room.

5. South transept and rose window.

6. The triforium.

7. The South ambulatory.

8. Foliated capital. Mid thirteenth century. Muniment Room.

9. Falcon capital. Mid thirteenth century. Muniment Room.

10. Triforium arch with stiff-leaf foliage and diapered spandrels.

11. Details of diaper and moulding of triforium arch in Apse.

12. Rich diaper. North transept.

13. Foliated arch springer.
South transept.

14. Head of master craftsman. North transept. Mid thirteenth century. Robert of Beverley or John of Gloucester?

15. Purbeck marble head over North transept door.
Mid thirteenth century. Edward I?

16. Corbel head. East triforium. Mid thirteenth century. Master Henry?

17. Corbel head of craftsman. East triforium. Mid thirteenth century.

18. Boss, naturalistic foliage (Vine). *c.*1280.
South aisle of the nave.

19. Boss, man torn by lions. Mid thirteenth century.
North aisle of the nave.

20. Boss, King David. Mid thirteenth century.
West aisle of the North transept.

21. Boss. Annunciation. Mid thirteenth century. North transept.

22. Boss, Combat between lion centaur and dragon.
Mid thirteenth century. Muniment Room.

23. Boss, combat between man and lion centaur.
Mid thirteenth century. Muniment Room.

24. Lancets in the Muniment Room.

25. Pilgrim and censing angel under rose window. South transept.

26. Censing angel. East corner. South transept.

27. Censing angel. West corner. South transept.
(Censer and hand broken off.)

28. Censing angel. East corner. South transept.

29. Painted stone heraldic shield. (Simon De Montfort.)
Mid thirteenth century. North aisle of the nave.

30. Angel choir. Mid thirteenth century. Soffit of lancet windows.
North transept.

31. St. Margaret emerging from dragon. Spandrel. North aisle of the nave.

32. Head of Abbot, triforium arch. South transept under rose window.

33. Corbel head. Mid thirteenth century (before and after cleaning). St. Faith's Chapel. 'The Dreaming Youth'.

34. Corbel head. Mid thirteenth century. St. Faith's Chapel.

35. Corbel head. Mid thirteenth century. St. Faith's Chapel.

36. Corbel head. Mid thirteenth century. St. Faith's Chapel.

37. Mural painting. Late thirteenth century. South transept.
Detail of Incredulity of St. Thomas.

38. Mural painting. Late thirteenth century. South transept.
Incredulity of St. Thomas.

39. Mural painting. Late thirteenth century. South transept.
St. Christopher.

40. Retable. Late thirteenth century. Central Panels.

41. Retable. Late thirteenth century. Detail of side panel.
The Feeding of the Five Thousand.

42. Coronation Chair. Back. (Prepared for the Coronation 1937.)

43. Coronation Chair.

44. Sedilia. *c.* 1300.

45. Sedilia. Painted wooden head of Abbot Walter de Wenlok?

46. Chapel of Our Lady of the Pew. North ambulatory.

47. Mural painting. Late fourteenth century. Muniment Room.
White Hart Badge of Richard II.

48. Henry V's Chantry Chapel. Detail showing Henry V on his charger.

49. Henry V's Chantry Chapel. Reredos. Fifteenth century.

50. Chapel of St. Edward the Confessor. Stone Screen. Fifteenth century. The vision of the drowning of the King of Denmark.

51. Chapel of St. Edward the Confessor. Stone Screen. Fifteenth century. The dedication of the Church.

52. Henry VII's Chapel. Apse during cleaning.

53. Henry VII's Chapel. South-East Apsidal Chapel
before war damage to modern glass.

54. Henry VII's Chapel. Sunlight and Sculpture.

55. Henry VII's Chapel. Side Chapel.

56. Henry VII's Chapel. Fan Vaulting.

57. Henry VII's Chapel. Fan Vaulting. North Aisle.

58. Henry VII's Chapel. Shield Supporter in Vestibule.

59. Henry VII's Chapel. Heraldic Leopard.

60. Henry VII's Chapel. St. Matthew and St. Luke, photographed when removed from their niches.

61. Henry VII's Chapel. St. Mary Magdalene and St. Anne, photographed when removed from their niches.

62. Henry VII's Chapel. St. Wilgefortis (Uncumber) and St. Jerome,
photographed when removed from their niches.

63. Stone Head of an Abbot (Abbot Islip?), early sixteenth century, in the Muniment Room.

64. Carved Rebus of Abbot Islip. Islip Chantry Chapel. Early sixteenth century. An eye and a slip. A boy slipping from a tree.